CHRISTINA MARTINOVIC

Tiny Paws, Big Surprises.

My Journey with a Toy Poodle

Contents

1 Introduction   1

2 Choosing and Being Chosen by Zach   3

3 The Learning Curve   6

4 Barking Beginnings   8

5 Training Tails with Zach   10

6 The Bond Deepens   12

7 Reflections on Parenthood   15

8 Advice for Future Toy Poodle Parents   18

9 Conclusion   24

1

Introduction

Welcome aboard "Tiny Paws, Big Surprises," your unofficial survival guide for life in the fast lane alongside a toy poodle. I'm Christina, and I've navigated the choppy waters of toy poodle guardianship with my furry co-pilot, Zacharie—or Zach, as we affectionately call him. Together, we've embarked on a journey filled with firsts: my initial foray into male pet ownership, laughably unsuccessful training sessions, and the rich emotional tapestry woven between a toy poodle and their human. Targeted at both experienced and first-time pet owners, this book draws from my experiences to deepen your understanding of the joys and challenges of raising these spirited, curly-coated pets.

Zach's grand entrance into my world was nothing short of a revelation, unearthing the steep, sometimes vertical, learning curve that comes with caring for a toy poodle. They're a breed apart, boasting a cocktail of sharp intelligence, endless zest, and emotional depths that could rival the Mariana Trench, offering unique challenges (and joys) unlike any other. My goal? To unfold the intricate layers of toy poodle parenthood, provide a playbook for gracefully navigating its highs and lows and maybe a little panache.

At the heart of our tale lies the twin pillars of patience and consistency, the unsung heroes in the quest to train a toy poodle. With brains that soak up new tricks like a sponge but bore as quickly as a teenager, keeping training sessions fresh and engaging is critical. Through our shared saga of victories and face-palms, this book will arm you with the strategies you need, tailor-made for your pint-sized Einstein.

What is the bond between humans and toy poodles? It's the stuff of legends, a theme we dive into with gusto. Zach has evolved from a mere pet to a cornerstone of my existence, a source of solace, camaraderie, and endless entertainment. Our story aims to spotlight the transformative power these little companions wield, enhancing your life in ways unimaginable.

So, as we set sail towards "Choosing and Being Chosen by Zach," consider this book your all-in-one compass and map for the delightful complexities of toy poodle guardianship. Merging real-life escapades, hands-on advice, and a deep dive into the unique bond shared with these remarkable creatures, "Tiny Paws, Big Surprises" is your indispensable companion on the road to becoming the ultimate toy poodle parent. Whether you're a seasoned dog enthusiast or considering adding a toy poodle to your family circus, this guide promises to be your north star to fostering a loving, vibrant home for your newest, fluffiest family member.

2

Choosing and Being Chosen by Zach

I n a world where "unprecedented times" became the year's catchphrase, along came Zach, my beacon of fluff and joy, defying the gloomy narrative of the early COVID-19 era. Picture this: a world grappling with the concept of social distancing, and there I was, about to close the distance between me and my future mischief-maker extraordinaire, Zach, nestled in the verdant paradise of Kauai, Hawaii. The universe was not without a sense of irony, aligning the stars and clearing the skies (and the airports) just in time for our grand meet-cute.

The moment Zach was handed to me, all 2.5 pounds of him, it was as if the universe whispered, "Here's the sitcom sidekick you never knew you needed." In that instant, an unspoken contract was formed, sealed with a paw shake and a look that said, "You're in for quite the ride, human." He was mine, and I was his, ready to navigate the uncharted waters of puppy parenthood together.

Zach, a mere nine weeks old, seemed to possess the serenity of a Zen master, sleeping through our journey back to Oahu with the grace of a seasoned traveler. As I watched him, a peaceful, snoring bundle of fur, I couldn't help but feel a rush of gratitude mixed with a dash of "What have I gotten myself into?" He was the epitome of perfection, a living, breathing, snuggling reminder of the good in the world.

Once home, Zach wasted no time declaring sovereignty over his new realm. Despite his compact stature, he was fearless, treating the backyard as his fiefdom to explore, conquer, and occasionally do his royal business. The mastery of the doggy door came quickly, an impressive feat and a mild forewarning of the shenanigans to come. His knack for learning wasn't just quick—it was Usain Bolt's quick, hinting at the whirlwind of intelligence and playful mayhem that defined our lives together.

Potty training was a breeze, or so I thought until Zach decided that puppy pads weren't just functional; they were fun! His new favorite game? "Capture the Pad," a spirited romp involving him prancing around the house with the pad in his mouth, leaving behind a confetti trail of what once was. His fascination didn't stop at puppy pads; oh no, toilet paper was the real treasure, each roll a potential victim of his playful plundering.

The bathroom became the scene of our most epic battles. A visitor merely reaching for some toilet paper would unknowingly trigger Zach's stealth mode, launching him into action. The heist of the toilet roll, followed by a triumphant dash, became his signature move. Watching him parade around, victorious, with his papery loot trailing behind, was a spectacle that could turn the grumpiest curmudgeon into a giggling fan. It was clear he relished these moments, his tiny tail wagging in triumph, a clear message that he had won yet another round of our ongoing playful skirmish.

In the grand tapestry of life's unexpected adventures, bringing Zach home was like stumbling upon a hidden doorway to a world filled with laughter, boundless energy, and, yes, a curious shortage of toilet paper. His arrival turned my life into an enchanting narrative of joy, challenges, and the kind of love that stories try to capture, but only hearts genuinely understand. Each day with Zach was a lesson in living in the moment, embracing the unexpected, and learning the fine art of puppy negotiation. With her wise, slightly prophetic warnings, my mother had seen the writing on the wall: "That little bundle of joy is going to keep you on your toes," she had said. And, as the days unfolded, her words echoed true, painting a picture of a life forever changed by the pitter-patter of tiny poodle feet.

But if you think the story ends with us mastering the art of toilet paper diplomacy and backyard explorations, think again. As we turned the page into Chapter 3, "The Learning Curve," it became apparent that the journey with Zach was only beginning. His early escapades were merely the opening act, a prelude to a symphony of lessons in patience, cunning, and the unexpected joys of toy poodle parenthood.

As we stepped into the next chapter, it was clear that Zach was not just a pet but a teacher in his own right, his every action a lesson, his every mistake a moment of learning—for both of us. From mastering the nuances of communication without words to navigating the challenges of training a willful yet incredibly intelligent companion, the path ahead promised to be as enriching as it was entertaining.

The stage was set, the players ready, and the adventure of a lifetime was about to take on new dimensions. Join us, won't you, as we dive headfirst into the wonders, the laughter, and the priceless lessons of Chapter 3.

3

The Learning Curve

As we rounded the corner from the whirlwind introduction of Zach into my life, detailed in the previous chapter, we were about to embark on what I affectionately call "The Learning Curve." This wasn't just a step into the next chapter of our adventure; it was more like stepping onto a rollercoaster without a seatbelt, blindfolded, with Zach at the controls.

Remember when I naively thought that having a male dog might not be so different? Zach quickly set me straight—each day with him has been a lesson in "Dog 101: The Male Poodle Edition." For starters, his marking antics turned our home into a tapestry of invisible spots only he seemed to cherish. Nightly, I found myself on hands and knees, flashlight in hand, embarking on a quest to uncover these hidden treasures. A friend suggested a black light for these expeditions, but I feared what I might discover would be worthy of a horror movie scene.

And then, there's Zach's intellect—a feature that should come with a warning label. Our backyard escapades often felt like tactical warfare, with him outmaneuvering me at every turn. I'm convinced he has a hidden stash of strategy guides he consults when I'm not looking. Occasionally, he'd graciously allow me a victory, ensuring our games remained appealing to his human. If Zach could talk, I imagine he'd offer a mix of sage advice and cheeky banter that would leave me both enlightened and utterly defeated.

Zach's understanding of "the cute look" could easily be his superpower. He wields it with the precision of a seasoned diplomat, securing treats and affection and occasionally bending the household rules to his will. It's a talent that ensures his place at the top of the household hierarchy, with the rest of us mere mortals eagerly awaiting his following command.

The grooming saga introduced a whole new level of drama to our lives. Transitioning from the perpetual shedding of a pug and a chocolate lab to the hypoallergenic curls of a toy poodle seemed like a dream come true. That dream, however, quickly evolved into a quest for the perfect groomer, capable of taming Zach's luxurious mane without triggering his dramatic disdain for paw handling. The journey through grooming misadventures, including a disastrous facial trim, taught us the importance of clear communication and finding a groomer who speaks 'poodle' fluently.

Through every trial and triumph, Zach has been my teacher, confidant, and source of endless joy. While occasionally testing the limits of my patience, his antics unveiled the depth of our bond—a bond built on mutual respect, a dash of cunning, and a lot of love. As we delve deeper into "The Learning Curve," it's clear that this journey is about more than just navigating the quirks of living with a toy poodle. It's about embracing the unexpected, learning to see the world through Zach's eyes, and discovering that, in the end, the most significant lessons come not from mastering the perfect sit or stay but from the heartwarming chaos of life with a poodle who has stolen my heart.

So, as we embark on this next chapter, let's fasten our seatbelts (figuratively speaking, because, remember, Zach is in charge) and prepare to dive deep into the lessons learned and the laughter shared.

4

Barking Beginnings

As we turn the page to Chapter 3, let's tune into the soundtrack of our journey with Zach—a series of spirited barks that herald the adventures and misadventures of life with a toy poodle whose vocal talents are as boundless as his energy. Zach, or as he's known in moments of mischief, "Sir Barks-a-Lot," has turned my life into an endless loop of surprises, most of which involve his vocal talents.

Zach's entry was like a fanfare, announcing his presence and a new way of living where silence is golden but rare. Among the many hats (or should I say collars?) toy poodles wear, the role of "Alert System Extraordinaire" was one Zach embraced with an enthusiasm I didn't see coming. This pint-sized guardian takes his job seriously, treating every rustle of leaves as a potential threat to national security. His bark, a sound of such magnitude it could quickly put opera singers to shame, has introduced me to decibels I hadn't known existed.

Adapting to the soundtrack of Zach's barking has been a journey. Attempting to desensitize him to everyday noises turned into lessons in futility, especially when I realized he responds to sounds I'm convinced are made by ghosts. His incredible alertness to the unusual, or frankly, to anything moving, is both admirable and, at 3 a.m., slightly less so.

Zach's audacious approach to home security comes with a small catch – his bravery is selective. Upon sounding the alarm, he promptly delegates the investigation duties to me, his trusty human sidekick. It's a dynamic that works: he barks, I check, and we both retreat (me, slightly embarrassed; him, entirely unbothered).

Navigating life with Zach has peeled back the layers on the complex personalities of toy poodles: fiercely loyal, unexpectedly loud, and with a courage that's, let's say, proportional to their size. Each day brings a deeper understanding and appreciation for the little guy, whose volume is matched only by his heart.

So, as we trot further into the journey of "Tiny Paws, Big Surprises," it becomes clear that this adventure is less about quieting the barks and more about tuning into the unique melody of life with a toy poodle. Zach's vocal performances, while not always music to my ears, are a constant reminder of the vibrant personality and protective spirit packed into his tiny frame.

Join us as we navigate the symphony of sounds, lessons in bravery (for both of us), and the unexpected joys from life with Zach. It's a story of love, laughter, and learning to appreciate the little things – even if they're often louder than anticipated.

Stick around for more tales from our journey. With Zach, there's always a new chapter waiting to be barked... I mean, penned.

5

Training Tails with Zach

Embarking on the training journey with Zach was like signing up for a roller coaster ride—exciting, daunting, and full of unexpected twists. Think of it as entering a game where the rules are made up, and the points don't matter, except the points do matter because every treat and every command is a step towards mutual understanding, or so I hoped.

Our first stop was the local big-box pet store, where dreams of a well-mannered pup are sold in aisle nine, between squeaky toys and organic dog food. These classes promised to turn your furry friend into a model citizen—think less wild child, more honor student. Only catch? We were in the middle of a pandemic, which turned our group classes into a socially distanced affair with all the intimacy of a Zoom call. The interaction was minimal, but on the bright side, Zach mastered the art of meaningful eye contact with other dogs from six feet away.

Taking Zach out felt like managing a tiny celebrity. Everywhere we went, he drew crowds, all amazed by his "impeccable" behavior. Little did they know that Zach was likelier to enroll in the school of creative chaos than to follow any strict behavioral code at home. His public persona was an act and a convincing one at that.

The real fun began with the treat-based motivation system—a method that Zach treated with all the enthusiasm of a cat faced with a closed door. To him, treats were less currency and more mild suggestions, hardly worth his time unless they involved something truly scandalous, like sneaking a lick of my ice cream cone when I wasn't looking.

Our graduation from pet store university (complete with a symbolic cap and gown) led us to the next level: doggy boot camp. Imagine sending your dog to a training retreat, hoping for a miracle. The reality was a mix of sleepless nights for me and, I imagine, a blend of confusion and adventure for Zach. When we reunited, and I was told to keep his leash on him indoors, it became clear who needed the training. With his best puppy dog eyes, Zach convinced me to ditch the leash, leaving me to wonder who was training whom.

This entire experience shed light on a crucial truth: training Zach was less about him learning to sit and stay and more about us learning to communicate and coexist harmoniously. It's a dance where sometimes you step on each other's toes, but you laugh it off and keep moving to the music.

So, as we wrap up this chapter, I've come to cherish the unscripted, imperfect moments of joy that come from life with Zach. He might not perform tricks on command, but he's taught me invaluable lessons about patience, love, and the beauty of embracing life's little quirks.

As we gear up for "The Bond Deepens," I'm armed with a bag of his favorite treats (for bribery or peace offerings, I haven't decided which) and a heart full of love for my adventurous, stubborn, and irreplaceable toy poodle. The best part of training? I discovered that sometimes the most meaningful lessons come not from perfect obedience but from the journey you take together, filled with love, laughter, and, yes, a bit of chaos.

6

The Bond Deepens

I f you've ever wondered what it's like to be shadowed by a fluffy, four-legged private investigator, welcome to my world. Zach, my red toy poodle, has elevated the term "mama's boy" to an art form, gluing himself to my side with an attachment so strong that it's as if he's monitoring my every move for signs of departure. This isn't just puppy love; it's a full-blown surveillance operation, and I'm the prime target.

Working from home has its perks, especially in the telework era, allowing Zach and me to spend nearly every waking moment together. It's a setup most dog owners would dream of, except for the tactical games of hide-and-seek that ensue whenever I attempt to put his harness on for a walk. He's got my routine down to a science, tracking my every move with the precision of a seasoned detective while maintaining an air of innocence that would fool anyone who doesn't know him as I do.

This bond we share is not just unique; it's transformative. A poodle, they say, becomes a part of you, and I couldn't agree more. Zach isn't just a pet; he's a piece of my heart walking around on four paws, embodying joy, mischief, and unconditional love in a way only a dog can.

My mind races with thoughts of him when we're apart: Is he on a secret marking mission? Engaging in a covert operation with paper towels? Or perhaps plotting his next playful ambush on an unsuspecting family member? The anticipation of returning home to his antics gets me through the day.

Our reunions are nothing short of cinematic. Picture this: I step into the house, the air charged with anticipation, only to find Zach poised around the corner, his rear end up in the air, ready to launch himself at me in a frenzy of joy. This little furball, charging at me like a missile of happiness, transforms me instantly. My voice shifts into that high-pitched, baby-talk register universally understood by pets worldwide. It's an involuntary reaction, a testament to the depth of our bond and his profound effect on me.

But let me share a little secret about how Zach plays the system. If he senses he's been alone for too long, he'll put on an Oscar-worthy performance of the "sick and pitiful" routine. He mopes around, projecting an aura of utter despair, manipulating my heartstrings with the skill of a master violinist. Yet, miraculously, at the mere sound of the treat drawer opening, he undergoes a transformation that would put Lazarus to shame, bounding over in seconds, all traces of his earlier "illness" gone. It's a ruse, a clever ploy, and I fall for it every time because he's Zach, and I'm just a mere human under the spell of his poodle magic.

This journey with Zach, this deepening bond, is more than just the antics, the games, and the unconditional love. It's about discovering the capacity for joy in the simple moments, the power of a bond that transcends words, and the realization that these moments with him are what truly matter in the grand scheme of life. As we navigate this adventure together, I'm constantly reminded of the unique, indescribable connection between a dog and their human—a bond forged in the warmth of shared experiences, laughter, and a few too many treats.

According to Zach, life is an endless series of moments to be cherished, lessons to be learned, and games to be played. And as his human, I'm just along for the ride, forever changed, endlessly amused, and deeply in love with my little shadow, my heart on four paws, my Zach.

7

Reflections on Parenthood

In the grand tapestry of life, where threads of countless colors and textures intertwine, adding a poodle to the mix is akin to introducing a vibrant splash of red that refuses to be ignored. Zach, my astute and ever-watchful poodle, has taught me that parenting a dog of his caliber is a journey marked by lessons in intelligence, empathy, and the kind of unconditional love books try to describe, but only the heart truly understands.

Zach's intelligence isn't just a trait; it's his superpower. The way he locks eyes with me, reading my every gesture and anticipating my next move, it's like living with a furry psychic. This isn't your garden-variety dog trick; this is a profound understanding of human emotion and intent that Zach possesses, an invisible bond that connects us without words. Witnessing the depth of connection that poodles share with their owners is nothing short of miraculous, a testament to the extraordinary companionship they offer.

The impact of Zach's presence in my life goes beyond mere companionship; it's a lesson in what it means to be needed and to need in return. He shadows me relentlessly, a constant reminder that no journey, not even from the couch to the fridge, is to be undertaken alone. His insistence on being by my side and his undivided attention to my every move speaks volumes of our bond—a bond that is not only felt but lived.

Every breed brings its unique flavor to the pet-parent relationship. Still, poodles, with their distinguished intelligence and striking personalities, offer a glimpse into what it might be like if our pets could converse with us, share jokes, or even debate the finer points of life. They exhibit a spectrum of emotions, quirks, and habits as rich and varied as humans. Embracing a pet, particularly one as expressive and demanding as a poodle, is an exercise in unconditional love. It's about accepting and cherishing the quirks, the unexpected expenses, and the endless anecdotes that come with them.

Parenting Zach has peeled back the layers of what it means to love unconditionally. It's about more than just providing a home; it's about creating a space where every quirk is celebrated, every expense is justified by the joy it brings, and every anecdote adds another layer to our complex, beautiful relationship. This journey has shown me that the essence of pet parenthood is not just caring for another being but allowing that being to illuminate parts of your heart you never knew existed.

As I reflect on this adventure of parenthood with Zach, I'm struck by the sheer magnitude of what it means to share your life with a poodle. It's a role filled with laughter, challenges, and an immeasurable depth of connection. With his penetrating stares and keen understanding, Zach has not just entered my life; he has transformed it, teaching me lessons in empathy, patience, and love that transcend the boundaries of what I thought possible.

In the end, the reflections on parenthood with a creature as captivating as Zach remind me daily of the beauty and complexity of life. They highlight our remarkable capacity to connect across species, communicate without words, and love beyond reason. This journey, with its ups and downs, its trials and triumphs, is not just about being a pet parent; it's about discovering the vast, uncharted territories of the heart, guided by the paws of a poodle who has become so much more than a pet—he's become my teacher, my companion, and my friend.

8

Advice for Future Toy Poodle Parents

Welcoming a toy poodle into your life is akin to embarking on an expedition filled with boundless joy, unforeseen challenges, and endless learning curves. With Zach as my intrepid companion, my journey through the landscape of toy poodle parenthood has been nothing short of a revelation, each day peppered with moments of hilarity, bewilderment, and lessons in unconditional love. This chapter aims to equip you, future poodle parents, with the compass and map I wish I had when I first set out on this adventure.

Preparations: Beyond Puppy-Proofing

Securing your home for a toy poodle, particularly one as inventively mischievous as Zach, isn't so much puppy-proofing as it is entering into a high-stakes game of hide and seek, where what you're hiding isn't yourself but every conceivable object that could potentially be turned into the focal point of Zach's next big adventure. Imagine, if you will, a world where toilet paper rolls become priceless artifacts to be discovered and kitchen towels are the flags of conquering heroes. This is the world, according to Zach, a realm where everything, absolutely everything, has the potential for play.

And it's about more than just securing the obvious hazards; that would be too easy. The innocuous items, the ones you wouldn't think so, often become the treasures most sought after in the excellent poodle quest. A lone sock left unattended? That's not laundry—that's a trophy. Is the corner of a rug slightly upturned? It's an invitation to dig to the other side of the world, or at least attempt to.

The excellent puppy pad escapade is a classic example. You might think, "Ah, here's a simple, effective solution to indoor bathroom needs." But in the eyes of a toy poodle, these pads are not so much for bathroom breaks as they are tickets to the most incredible show on Earth. Zach, in his infinite wisdom and boundless enthusiasm, sees each pad as an opportunity for performance art. The act of shredding, dragging, and parading these pads around the house is not mere play; it's a statement, a declaration of the joy of being alive and young and possessing teeth.

Watching Zach in action, one can't help but marvel at this tiny creature's sheer energy, creativity, and undeniable charisma. Each race through the hallways, each pad flapping behind him like a superhero's cape, reminds us of the boundless joy and unfettered spirit that dogs, especially toy poodles, bring into our lives. It's a spectacle, yes, but also a lesson—a lesson in finding happiness in the simplest things, turning the mundane into the extraordinary, and living each moment with gusto and unabashed enthusiasm.

Preparing your home and your heart for a toy poodle is to embrace this spirit and recognize that while the physical preparations are essential, the emotional readiness to join in the game, laugh at the chaos, and celebrate the spontaneous eruptions of joy is what truly matters. It's about understanding that life with a toy poodle is not just about managing their energy but about allowing their zest for life to invigorate your own, to see the world anew through their eyes, where every day is an adventure waiting to happen. No matter how mundane, every object is a treasure waiting to be discovered.

So as we move forward, arm yourself not just with puppy-proof locks and gates but with a sense of humor, a reservoir of patience, and an open heart ready for the love, laughter, and, yes, a bit of chaos that a toy poodle like Zach brings into your life. In these moments of shared joy and playful discovery, we find not just the true essence of living with a toy poodle but the deeper, more profound realization of the beauty of life itself, unfettered, unscripted, and utterly magnificent.

The Quest for the Perfect Groomer

Embarking on the quest for the perfect groomer for Zach, my toy poodle extraordinaire turned out to be more epic than I'd initially anticipated. It's one thing to admire poodle fur in all its glory—curly, soft, and seemingly designed by Mother Nature on a particularly creative day. It's quite another to maintain it. Picture trying to keep a cloud perfectly fluffed and pristine while it explores mud puddles and indulges in the occasional trash can dive. That's the daily reality of poodle ownership for you.

Finding a groomer who could navigate the complexities of Zach's luxurious mane was akin to searching for a unicorn. You see, poodle fur isn't just hair; it's a statement, a lifestyle, a testament to the breed's regal origins. It demands not just a groomer but a fur artist who understands that beneath that sophisticated exterior beats the heart of a dog as likely to roll in something unspeakable as they are to strut down the living room runway.

Our search was exhaustive, spanning the spectrum from boutique salons where the shampoo smelled more expensive than my own to no-frills establishments where the main selling point was the sheer speed of their clippers. Along the way, we encountered groomers of all philosophies. Some treated Zach like a delicate sculpture, while others seemed to think they were shearing a sheep rather than crafting the perfect poodle pompadour.

Finding that perfect blend of skill, care, and chemistry took time. A good groomer, as I learned, is more akin to a partner in crime (the crime being attempting to keep a toy poodle looking dignified in all situations). They're part therapist, part artist, and part Zen master, capable of soothing canine and human nerves. It's about more than just avoiding mats and tangles; it's about ensuring Zach's health and happiness, about preserving the dignity of a dog who carries himself with the self-assuredness of royalty but who isn't above chasing his tail with abandon.

Communicating our needs and preferences became a critical part of the process, especially regarding more... delicate matters. Zach, for instance, made it abundantly clear that certain grooming practices were not to his liking. The revelation that skipping the dreaded anal gland expression made him a more cooperative client was a game-changer. Suddenly, grooming sessions transformed from tense standoffs to occasions of mutual respect and understanding, with Zach emerging not just looking like a show dog but feeling like one too—proud, pampered, and ready to take on the world.

Ultimately, the quest for the perfect groomer taught me as much about patience and communication as it did about poodle hair care. It underscored the importance of finding someone who had the technical skills and the right approach and attitude, who saw Zach not as just another appointment on their schedule but as the unique individual he is.

So, as we continue our journey together, with many more grooming sessions on the horizon, I'm grateful for the lessons learned and the relationships formed. The quest for the perfect groomer, like the broader adventure of pet parenthood, is filled with unexpected challenges and rewards. It's a testament that the most critical aspects of care—whether for poodles or people—lie not in the tools or techniques but in the understanding, compassion, and connection that bloom in the most unexpected places.

Embracing the Unexpected: The Heart of Toy Poodle Parenthood

Diving into the world of toy poodle parenting with Zach is like signing up for an improv comedy class where the instructor is a fluffy, four-legged genius with a flair for the dramatic and a penchant for sock thievery. It's a life less ordinary, where every day unfolds like a sitcom, filled with laughter, plot twists, and the occasional cliffhanger (usually involving the whereabouts of my favorite socks).

Zach's escapades, from his meticulously planned sock heists to his soap opera-worthy reactions to bath time, have turned my journey into toy poodle parenthood into a vibrant tapestry of unexpected joys and trials. Each sock unearthed from his secret stash, each dramatic sigh as he resigns himself to grooming, adds a splash of color to this tapestry, reminding me daily of the joys and challenges of living with such a spirited creature.

These experiences have crystallized the true essence of life with a toy poodle: a roller coaster ride of emotions, from the highs of shared laughter to the lows of shared stubbornness. Every new day comes a fresh adventure, a new lesson in the art of patience (or the art of locating hidden socks), and countless opportunities to strengthen the bond with my furry sidekick. Embracing each moment with an open heart and a ready laugh is vital, for it's within these spontaneous, unscripted episodes that the heart of pet parenthood truly beats.

Final Thoughts: Charting Your Course

As you stand on the threshold of the toy poodle world, arm yourself not just with the essentials—leashes, toys, treats—but with an arsenal of patience, a reservoir of love, and a boundless capacity for wonder. The path ahead is dotted with moments of sheer joy, interspersed with challenges designed to test your mettle and deepen your bond with your new companion.

But fear not, future poodle parents, for these trials and tribulations are merely stepping stones to forging an unbreakable bond with your poodle—a bond characterized by mutual affection, understanding, and a shared zest for life. This unique, enduring connection promises to enrich every facet of your existence, painting your world with the vibrant hues of unconditional love and companionship.

To those brave adventurers poised to embark on this remarkable voyage into the realm of toy poodle parenthood: may your journey be illuminated by the warm glow of laughter, infused with the depth of love, and accompanied by the unparalleled companionship of your new furry confidant. Welcome to a life redefined by wonder, where every day invites you to embrace the unexpected and find joy in the journey.

So, lace up your walking shoes, stock up on those irresistibly squeaky toys, and prepare your heart for the arrival of your toy poodle. The adventure that awaits is one of growth, discovery, and a love so profound it transcends words. Welcome to the enchanting, exhilarating world of toy poodle parenthood. Your grand adventure begins now.

9

Conclusion

As I sit down to pen the concluding chapter of this whirlwind adventure called toy poodle parenthood, Zach—my constant shadow, my four-legged muse—curls up beside me, his presence a silent testament to our journey together. It's a journey that has transformed me in ways I could never have imagined, etching an indelible mark upon my heart and reshaping my world with every mischievous antic, every moment of shared silence, and every lesson learned the hard way.

Reflecting on this journey, I'm struck by the profound truth that bringing a toy poodle into your life is less about owning a pet and more about welcoming a new soul into your family. Zach, with his boundless energy, intelligence that borders on sassy, and capacity for love that seems to know no bounds, has been more than just a companion; he has been a teacher, friend, and source of endless inspiration.

The path of toy poodle parenthood is fraught with challenges, to be sure. From the early days of puppy-proofing to the ongoing adventures in training, grooming, and simply coexisting with a creature of such intelligence and will, there have been moments of frustration, doubt, and sheer exasperation. Yet, for every moment of challenge, countless more have been filled with joy, laughter, and a love so pure it defies description.

This journey has taught me the true meaning of patience, unconditional love, and the beauty of embracing life's unexpected moments. Zach's antics—whether he's orchestrating a daring escape with a roll of toilet paper or giving me that look that says he's about to do something he knows he shouldn't—have not only tested my limits but have also opened my heart and filled my life with a joy I never knew was missing.

My advice to those embarking on this journey is simple: embrace every moment. The days may sometimes be long, but the years are short, and before you know it, the tiny ball of fur that once fit in your palm will have grown into an irreplaceable member of your family. Cherish the early mornings, the late-night cuddles, the unexpected showers of affection, and even the moments of mischief—they are the threads that weave the tapestry of your life together.

Prepare yourself for a journey that will challenge you, change you, and ultimately enrich your life in ways you cannot imagine. Know that the road ahead is filled with laughter, love, and the occasional mystery stain, but every step of the way, your toy poodle will be there, looking up at you with eyes full of adoration, ready to take on the world together.

In conclusion, the journey of toy poodle parenthood is an adventure of the heart, a voyage that will take you through the highest and lowest highs, only to emerge on the other side with a forever changed heart. As I look down at Zach, now sleeping peacefully beside me, I am reminded that this journey, with all its trials and triumphs, is not just about the moments we share but about the love that binds us, unspoken but unbreakable.

So, to those about to step into the world of toy poodle parenthood, I extend my heartfelt wishes for a journey filled with love, laughter, and the kind of happiness that only a toy poodle can bring. Welcome to the family.